The GEOLOGY
of Denali National Park *&* Preserve

Text *&* Photography by Michael Collier

Alaska Geographic Association
Anchorage, Alaska

Alaska Geographic Association thanks Denali National Park and Preserve
for their assistance in developing and reviewing this publication. Alaska Geographic
(formerly known as Alaska Natural History Association) works in partnership with
the National Park Service to further public education and appreciation for national
parks in Alaska. The publication of books, among other activities, supports and
complements the National Park Service mission.

Text and Photography: Michael Collier
Editorial: Ruth Reitmeier
Design: Christina Watkins
Production: Sandra Fulmer
Illustrations: Peter Corrao, pages 12, 32, 35 & 41

ISBN: 978-0-930931-04-9

Alaska Geographic Association is a nonprofit educational partner of Alaska's
parks, forests and refuges. In addition to publishing books and other materials
about Alaska's public lands, Alaska Geographic offers field-based educational
programs, teacher trainings and operates visitor center bookstores. The net
proceeds from publication sales support educational programs that connect
people to the natural and cultural heritage of Alaska's public lands.
For more information or to become a supporting member:
www.alaskageographic.org

Alaska
Geographic
241 North C Street
Anchorage, Alaska 99501
www.alaskageographic.org

CONTENTS

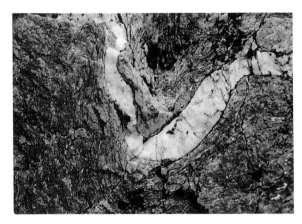

*Schist with quartz intrusion
above the Savage River.*

INTRODUCTION

ONE AFTERNOON I committed one of those little faux pas that, taken collectively, make the world a more perplexing place to live. "Why," I asked a friend, "would anyone come to Denali, but to see the mountain?" My friend is an Alaskan hunting guide, a man who truly knows animals. He and his wife—thinking no doubt of bears, moose, caribou, sheep, wolves, lions and tigers—stared at me across a gulf as wide as all outdoors. There was no point in trying to take my foot out of my mouth. That's just the way the world works: some folks come to Denali to see the mountain, and others to see the animals.

Mount McKinley—20,320 feet above sea level. The mountain leaps 18,000 feet above the surrounding countryside, an abrupt rise of a magnitude to rival any other mountain in the world. The highest point in North America. Denali—a mountain of enigmatic geology and uncertain origins, caught in a gridlock of faults and thrusts. A mountain so massive as to make any geologist sit up and forget all the world's lions and tigers, bears and wolves—at least until they come nosing around his camp.

OPPOSITE:
Denali sunrise above the McGonagall Mountains.

Because the geology is complex, learning about the mountain—its rocks and their history—is a slow process. But, as with all searches, there are moments when the light is just right and the world seems clear as crystal. I had just finished lunch one afternoon on a pass above the upper Toklat River; I was laying on my back, out of the wind. It struck me that I would eventually have to climb down a thousand feet, just to get to tundra. A thousand feet between me and the nearest carpet of plants—and tundra at that. Rock everywhere was unobscured, all brown and white and yellow, warm with the morning's sunlight. A bank of clouds shot through the pass like surf breaking against a shore, temporarily obscuring the sun. After the clouds had passed, the rocks were again suffused with a glow as if from within. Denali, for the moment, was a land reduced to the purest essentials—sky and rock.

But the view of Denali isn't always so clear. The geology of southern Alaska is a tangled mesh of differing types of rock, interwoven faults and folds, all set within a terrain so jumbled that geologic field trips are regularly transformed into major expeditions. Tangled enough to make some folks wish they'd gotten interested in those lions and tigers after all.

Rocks at Denali seem to come and go, to change from one type to another within just a few feet. In fact, geologists themselves can't agree about a lot of fundamental aspects of Denali geology. Just when you think you understand one scientist's point, somebody else comes along and tells you that it isn't so. Don't be discouraged. Some facts are as solid as rock, and out of the arguments there emerges a story that is beginning to explain Alaskan geology, Denali geology. A story that is rewriting the geologic history of all of western North America.

To tell the story briefly: in 1980 a few geologists proposed that the entire western edge of North America had been shuffled about much more than previously suspected. According to these geologists, entire 'terranes'—thousands of miles long, hundreds wide—had been rearranged like pieces in a colossal jigsaw puzzle, generally moving northward relative to the rest of the continent. And there sits Mount McKinley, at the northern apex of all this motion. But before digging into these stories, it would be wise to back up, take a deep breath, and get a running start. . . . .

EARLY DAYS

THE KOYUKON PEOPLE, an Athabascan tribe living in the valleys of the Yukon River, tell a story about Raven from their Distant Time. Raven had made advances upon a certain young lady but met with little success. Out of spite, he dispatched her from his canoe to the bottom of a lake, and doing so, brought down the understandable wrath of his would-be mother-in-law. She loosed her two grizzlies upon the Raven. He paddled furiously away as the bears dug at the lake's edge, raising waves that were certain to swamp his canoe. Raven hurled his harpoon into the waves; it glanced off a low wave and lodged farther south in a much greater one. The waves were turned to stone—the first a set of low hills, the second a great mountain that would be called Deenaalee. And Raven, that devil, got away.

The mountain has not come by its name easily. It has been variously called Denali by the Athabascans, Doleyka by the Susitna tribes, and Traleyka by people of the Cook Inlet area. The Russians knew it as Bulshaia Gora. Frank Densmore led an 1889 prospecting party from the Tanana River to the Kuskokwim regions; his enthusiastic descriptions of the mountain engendered the name 'Densmore's Peak,' in common usage along the Yukon until the end of the century.

William A. Dickey was a displaced Seattle merchant who trooped up the Susitna River in 1896. His account of the trip, published by the *New York Sun* in January the following year, included the first map to use the name "Mount McKinley." Dickey later explained that he had run into two Alaskan prospectors who made such a fuss about a silver-based currency that he retaliated by naming the mountain after William McKinley, a presidential candidate who staunchly supported the gold standard. For better or worse, the name stuck by virtue of its 1897 publication in the *Sun*.

The first recorded steps carved into Mount McKinley were made with a geologist's pick. Alfred H. Brooks had been commissioned by the United States Geological Survey to traverse the region from Cook Inlet to the Yukon River— 800 trackless miles of bog, forest, and mountain. From a base camp near Slippery Creek, Brooks struck out alone on August 6, 1902 for the northern flank of Mount McKinley. He reached an altitude of 7500 feet before hunger eroded his resolve to go higher. Brooks was hounded by those nagging doubts that haunt every solo climber: "With the aid of my geologic pick I managed to cut steps in the slippery surface, and thus climbed a hundred feet higher; then the angle of slope became steeper, and as the ridge on which the glacier lay fell off at the sides in sheer cliffs, a slip would have been fatal." These thoughts didn't prevent him from publishing an article the following year in the *National Geographic* Magazine, entitled "Plan for Climbing Mount McKinley."

Alfred Brooks was more than an adventurer. He was the first of a few distinguished early geologists who explored and mapped the Denali area. Brooks' initial large-scale map and subsequent work in the Kantishna mining district still stand as classic scientific investigations. In addition to Brooks, S.R. Capps and John Reed were among a handful of those pioneer geologists whose work was so aptly described by Pierre St. Amand in a classic 1957 paper on the Denali Fault: "Field work in this general region proceeds very slowly because of the great topographic relief, the difficulties in provisioning and transporting parties, and in keeping alive while the work is being done."

Kantishna mining district.
Photo courtesy NPS.

Keeping alive, indeed. Despite the difficulties, Alaska at the turn of the century was a place and time to be alive. Opportunity sprang from behind every shadow. For instance, Felix Pedro struck gold in 1902 and Fairbanks sprouted overnight. Judge James Wickersham established a new federal court there in the spring of 1903; in a matter of weeks he was seduced off into the wilderness, tantalized by Mount McKinley's presence to the south. He booked passage on the *Tanana Chief*, which became the first steamer to push into the lower reaches of the Kantishna River. In a headlong rush to scale the mountain, the Wickersham party stumbled across gold in Chitsia Creek, a Kantishna tributary, and staked mining claims in the area almost as an afterthought. Though the Wickersham party's ascent was stymied by vertical walls of ice at the 8000-foot level, the trip would have far-reaching effects. Back in Fairbanks, the judge was questioned as much about his Chitsia Creek claims as about the attempted climb.

Joseph Dalton and Joseph Quigley prospected along the Toklat River in 1904, producing minor shows of color. The next summer Quigley and partner Jack Horn panned paying placer streaks on Glacier Creek, another Kantishna tributary. By mid-July, the first of two or three thousand stampeders were crawling like locusts through the Kantishna Hills, up every drainage of the placer-bearing streams. Within weeks, six new towns had sprung up in a forty-mile circle. But opportunity is too often a stranger to prosperity. The thin shows

Joe and Fanny Quigley, John Busia placer mining near Kantishna.

Photo courtesy NPS.

of bonanza gold were quickly exhausted; one year later, the towns were empty and most of the would-be miners were gone.

A few stayed on. Joe Quigley had come into the country by way of the Chilkoot Trail in 1891. His Last Chance Mine on Caribou Creek produced paying amounts of antimony; he also found lead, zinc, silver, gold, and copper on what would eventually be known as Quigley Ridge. In 1920 Joe and his wife Fannie were the first to stake claims on Copper (Eielson) Mountain; others joined them, but none could overcome the economic handicap of shipping ore so far to market—by horse and sled in wintertime to the Kantishna River where it was stockpiled until spring breakup, then by steamer down the Tanana and Yukon rivers, and finally by sea to the mill at Tacoma, Washington.

Gold in the ground will always be too much for some folks to bear. Placer deposits along creeks with such optimistic names as Eldorado and Eureka continued to pay slow steady returns for the hard work of surface miners. A dredge on Caribou Creek was producing two or three hundred ounces of gold a week just before the Second World War. Earl Pilgrim developed a twenty-six-foot-wide vein of high-grade stibnite along Stampede Creek that was in production until 1970. Potato-size nuggets of gold still turn up every once in a while in the spoil piles around Kantishna.

But times change. The Kantishna Hills were annexed into Denali National Park in 1978; mining was halted by court order in 1985 while the Park Service evaluated the effect of mining on the surrounding environment. I flew out to Kantishna and talked awhile with folks thereabouts. Predictably, I found that feelings run high on both sides of the mining question. Walking from the roadhouse back out to the airstrip, I found myself inspecting any rock that sparkled or was even smudged with yellow. Some things never change. I thought I could hear Joe Quigley laughing at me from just beyond the creek.

GLACIERS

ONE BRIGHT AUGUST MORNING, a blue and red Cessna (with skis where God meant wheels to be) descended toward the Southeast Fork of the Kahiltna Glacier. The altimeter read 7500 feet. 7200. Flaps down. Slowed to 60 knots. 7100. Sky almost as deep a blue as the plane; a few brown rocks visible. Otherwise the surrounding world was everywhere white. 7050 feet. The skis touched and the plane raised a snowy rooster-tail as it spun around to a stop. I stepped onto the glacier and unloaded my tent. With a good-bye waggle of its wings, the plane disappeared and the echoes of its engine were lost in the distance. I took a deep breath and looked around. This was the Kahiltna Base Camp, where most climbers begin their ascent of Mount McKinley. But it was very late in the climbing season and I was the only soul around.

To set the record straight, I am not a mountain climber. Furthermore,

Glaciers flowing out of the Alaska Range carve deep U-shaped valleys, and carry vast quantities of rock plucked from the sides of the mountains. Crevasses typically form where the glacier flows over a hump in the underlying bedrock.

by August, glacier travel becomes quite a poor idea as crevasses yawn open, reemerging from their mantle of last winter's snow. Glaciers are rivers of ice. They move *from* places where snow accumulates faster than it can melt, *to* places where the snow melts faster than it can accumulate. As the Kahiltna—or any other glacier—creeps down its valley, the ice is alternately squeezed and stretched while negotiating bends and bumps along the way. For the most part, glacial ice behaves as a plastic material, actually flowing around obstacles. But occasionally, the corners are too tight or the ice falls are too steep, and the ice is torn. The once-smooth surface of the glacier cracks open as a crevasse. Crevasses can be an inch wide, or they can be tens of feet wide and a couple of hundred feet deep. Some appear narrow at the surface, only to widen into cathedral-sized chasms below.

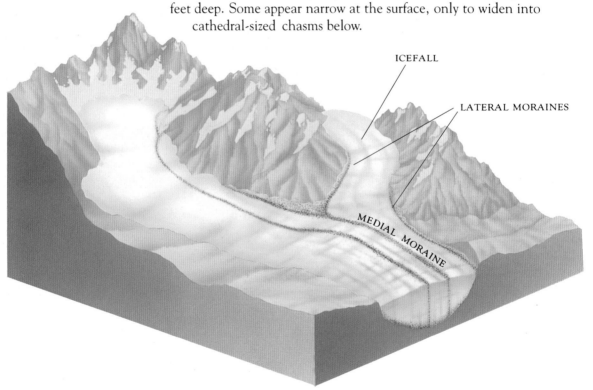

ICEFALL

LATERAL MORAINES

MEDIAL MORAINE

Alone, I was perfectly happy to sit for days square on the middle of that glacier with many hundreds of feet of ice between my tent and the nearest solid rock. Looming above were Mount Hunter and Mount Foraker. Mount McKinley's summit, eight miles distant, was two-and-a-half miles above my perch on the Southeast Fork of the Kahiltna. With the day's warmth, ice and rock began to crash down the valley walls in a continuously building crescendo.

The Ruth Glacier near Glacier Point.

I watched as a block of ice the size of a gas station broke from a high ridge on Hunter and cascaded down the northwest face; it ricocheted off a ledge and into space, trailing snow in a veil two thousand feet long. After sunset, silence descended as the walls froze once again. Mount McKinley lingered last of all, bathed in pale orange light. I fell asleep and dreamed I was flying.

Surprisingly, some fifty percent of Alaska shows no evidence of having ever been glaciated. The Yukon Valley remained ice-free during the cold

14

Stream cutting into the
Cantwell Formation south of
Polychrome Pass.

Pleistocene epoch (from about 2,500,000 until 8000 years before present), even though to the south Alaska was in the grips of successive glacial advance-and-retreat cycles. The reason for this difference can be found in the great arc of the Alaska Range. These mountains have always acted as a barrier to storms sweeping in from the northern Pacific; as a result, snow and ice pile up on the south while the north remains cold but relatively dry. One glance at a modern map of Denali shows great ice fields to the south of the Alaska Range, but only a few individual glaciers venturing down from the north side of the range.

Geologist Clyde Wahrhaftig spent a good deal of time during the 1950s examining glacial terraces above the Nenana River. He sorted out evidence that suggested four major glacial pulses. The earliest and most extensive was the Browne Glaciation, which took place roughly 2,000,000 years ago. Lobes of glacial deposits—a potpourri of large and small rocks from many miles away—were spewed down the Nenana River, stretching thirty miles north of Denali Park Depot, and also down the lower stetches of the Savage River. Next was what Wahrhaftig called the Dry Creek Glaciation, occurring perhaps 200,000 years ago. Evidence of this episode is so poorly preserved that some geologists have even questioned its existence. Deposits from both of these early glacial pulses have been subsequently tilted by the ongoing uplift of the Alaska Range.

Better documentation exists for the Healy Glaciation which got underway some 70,000 years ago. Ice poured out of the Alaska Range, coalescing into a sheet that stretched over most of southern Alaska. During that period, the Nenana Glacier flowed mostly to the south, but an arm did spill over the Alaska Range to the north, gouging a course through the mountains that the Nenana River now follows. The Nenana Glacier that exists today to the east of the Park is but a shadow of its former self, now restricted to a much smaller area near its source in the Alaska Range.

As this third glacial pulse waned, it dumped a poorly sorted load of stones, boulders, and other debris, called a 'terminal moraine,' at its retreating foot near the present-day town of Healy. The moraine blocked the Nenana River channel, forming prehistoric Lake Moody. The lake filled with mud, and the river eventually cut a new channel to escape through what is now a particularly steep-walled section of the Nenana River Gorge.

The Riley Creek Glaciation wrote the final chapter in the Pleistocene story of Denali. It took place by fits and starts, in four episodes from 25,000 to 9500 years ago; none were as extensive as any of those previously mentioned. During these advances, the Nenana Glacier managed to extend only about as far as Denali Park Depot on Riley Creek, before shrinking back to its present position high in the Alaska Range.

It's the rare corner of Denali National Park that has not been marked by the passage or presence of ice. I seriously doubt that a shuttle bus driver has ever gotten beyond the Savage River Bridge without informing his charges that the U-shaped valley upstream was carved by a glacier and the V-shaped valley downstream was carved by a stream. True enough.

Glacial erratic—a granite boulder dropped above Hines Creek by a now-withdrawn glacier.

Other evidence of past glacial activity can be found near Polychrome Pass. Here the foothills of the Alaska Range stretch like fingers down from the south, each manicured by its private glacier. The valleys between the ridges now hold rock glaciers—piles of rock with cores of ice, gradually creeping downhill.

Another example of the impact of glaciers on Denali is visible from the Park Headquarters area, where two odd rocks stand twinned against the southwestern horizon. They are house-sized pieces of granite where granite really ought not be. 'Erratics,' they're called, rolled into place by the nuzzlings of a now-retreated glacier. I recommend a hike to them in late August when the blueberries are ripe, about hand-level as you climb up the forty-degree slope.

Eielson Visitor Center commands a fine view of the huge Muldrow Glacier. But more than one visitor has asked, "What glacier?" A fair question, since the Muldrow is black as it reaches the McKinley Bar. The ice is covered by a two-foot veneer of rock and soil, and sports a vigorous growth of alder and willow. Even though its lower reaches look a bit downtrodden, the Muldrow is not a glacier with which to trifle. It sweeps forty miles down from the highest north-facing flanks of Mount McKinley, gathering the Traleika and Brooks glaciers into its folds along the way.

In its day, the Muldrow washed up onto the Kantishna Hills; a beached block of its ice remained to form the cast of Wonder Lake, twelve miles beyond

The somewhat dirty terminus of the Muldrow Glacier.

the glacier's present terminus. In 1956 sections of the Muldrow surged forward, rumbling along as fast as 1100 feet per day; it advanced more than four miles before returning to relative dormancy in 1957. Swirls imprinted in the moraines below the Muldrow's confluence with the Traleika and Brooks glaciers tell of such surges having occurred three other times in the past two hundred years. Not a trifling glacier. All the same, if it were my glacier with that thatch of alder and willow, I'd mow it.

Glaciers, and the rivers that flow as melt-water from their bases, have a truly amazing capacity to carry rock from one place to another—indeed, to move mountains. Water that pours from the base of Sunset Glacier can be milky grey, colored by rock that has been ground to powder by the inexorable ice. In flood, the water carries larger particles of sand, cobbles, even the odd boulder at high stages.

Sunrise and Gorge creeks join Sunset Creek just as it begins to meander across a wide plain that stretches below Eielson—the Thorofare, it's appropriately called. Five miles long, a couple miles wide, and fairly flat, the Thorofare acts as a hiker's switchyard: sooner or later anyone who hikes very often in Denali will cross the Thorofare. (Ben Eielson, that shooting star of early Alaskan aviation, landed on the Thorofare around the corner from Glacier Creek and the Muldrow in 1924. Mount Eielson, once called Copper Mountain, was renamed in his honor after he died in a plane crash in 1929.)

On a June afternoon, the Thorofare River can be difficult to cross. The current isn't just strong: it's hypnotizing. One's footing is unseen and forever shifting. In places, the river flows as a single channel thigh-deep to a tall man; in others the water fans out, inches deep over a wide area. The thread of the current weaves in and around itself, repeatedly braiding and unraveling. This braided pattern is the result of an excess of sediment, supplied by the inexhaustible glaciers back upstream.

OPPOSITE:
Braided stream pattern of the McKinley River bar below the terminus of the Muldrow Glacier.

At no time (as far as we can tell) has the Thorofare ever run bank to bank. As soon as the current scoops out a nice clean channel, some sediment-laden flood will come booming down to clog things up, turning the current out into a new path. Over time, the river migrates back and forth, like a shepherd trying to herd an unruly flock— running here, now there, trying to get all its cobbles moved on down the mountain. Taken in a geologic context, our lifetime is like the shutter of a fast camera—its short span freezes the sand and cobbles of the Thorofare, leaves them hanging in suspended animation. But taken in a larger context, the rocks are in a headlong rush from the mountains down to the sea.

Cobbles paving the Thorofare below Eielson Visitors Center.

It strikes me that the Thorofare would be hard on a geologist with a bad hangover. Walking along, a mile from tundra and five miles from trees, he would have nothing but rocks to think about. That cobble is limestone. That one granite. That one gneiss. Phyllite. Metarhyolite, actinolytic schist, radiolarian

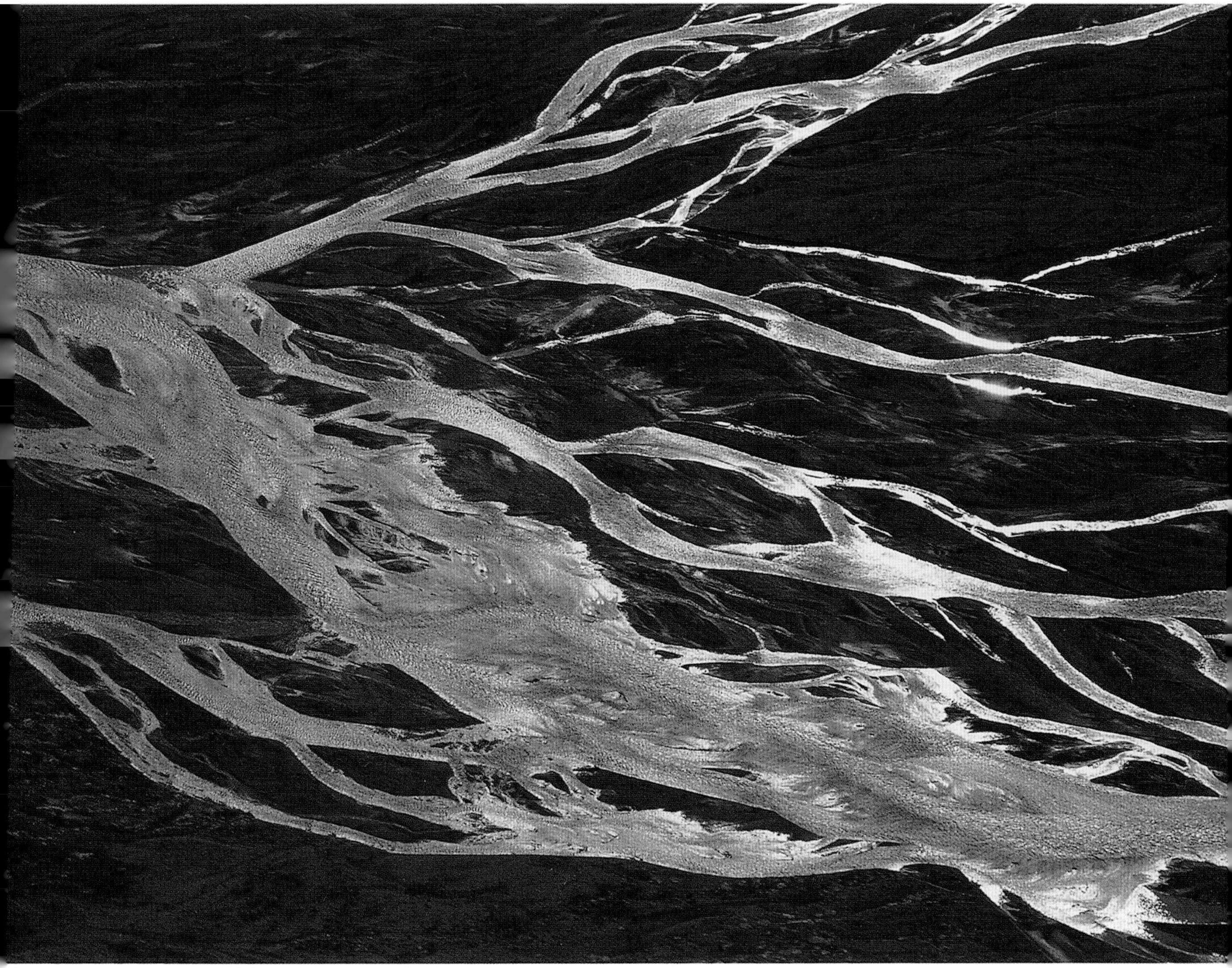

chert, and oh god there's graywacke. Micaceous sandstone, green tuff, serpentinite, gabbro, argillite, granodiorite, and before you know it, he's got a headache that no amount of aspirin is going to fix.

The obvious question is: how did so many different kinds of rock get put into one little stream channel? Time to back up again, and attend to a few fundamentals.

ROCKS

IN ALL THE WORLD, there are only three basic kinds of rock. Sedimentary. Igneous. Metamorphic. At times the wisest geologist would be hard pressed to come up with any finer distinctions about a given suite of rocks. To learn just these three types is to gain a foothold on the rest of geology. Sedimentary: rock formed from sediments, laid down by wind or water. Igneous: rock that has cooled and crystallized from molten material. Metamorphic: rock that used to be something else, and changed (without melting) in response to temperature and pressure.

In the greatest sense, there is nothing new under the sun. Since the beginning of geologic history, the earth has been recycling one rock into another. Sedimentary rocks get squeezed and baked into metamorphic rocks which later are dragged deep into the earth where they melt, cool to become igneous rocks which later are eroded away, forming grains of sand or silt which get cemented somewhere else into a sedimentary rock. Time goes on.

Which brings up another matter: geologic time. The earth has been shuffling its rocks around for quite a while. Early geologists dated formations by comparing fossils found in the rocks. A phenomenally intricate system of fossil

Era	Period		Epoch	Millions of years ago
CENOZOIC	Quaternary		Pleistocene	1.6
	Neo-gene		Pliocene	5.3
		Tertiary	Miocene	23.7
	Paleo-gene		Oligocene	36.6
			Eocene	57.8
			Paleocene	66.4
MESOZOIC	Cretaceous			
				144
	Jurassic			
				208
	Triassic			225
PALEOZOIC	Permian			
				286
	Pennsylvanian			
				320
	Mississippian			
				360
	Devonian			
				408
	Silurian			438
	Ordovician			
				505
	Cambrian			
				570
PRECAMBRIAN				

Geologic Time

identification and stratification allowed geologists to decide whether a given rock had been formed during an age before the appearance of life (Precambrian), an age of old forms of life (Paleozoic), middle forms (Mesozoic), or recent forms of life (Cenozoic). Splitters not lumpers, the paleontologists who engineered this scheme went on to further subdivide each era into many finer periods and epochs.

The *comparative* system outlined above (capable only of describing one rock as older or younger than another) was unable to give *absolute* dates. Geologists subsequently learned to use constant radioactive decay rates to measure geologic time in years. Potassium-argon, rubidium-strontium, and radiocarbon dating methods are all based on the measurement of ridiculously tiny amounts of these parent materials and their break-down products in specific rocks. As a result, we can assign absolute ages to the eras mentioned above. Precambrian—before 570 million years ago. Paleozoic—570 to 225 million years ago. Mesozoic—225 to 65 million years. And Cenozoic—65 million years right up to the present. And the earth itself appears to be a bit more than four-and-a-half billion years old.

So much for theory and background. It's time to put on our sneakers, get outside, and look at a few rocks. One of the Park's more easily identified sedimentary rocks is the

Nenana Gravel. It forms low hills south of the Park road between the Savage and Sanctuary rivers. Occasionally a roadcut or stream bank will dissect out a nice exposure of this tan rock, composed of many small pebbles, typically two or three inches in diamater. Scuff the rock with a boot and its poorly cemented pebbles easily crumble apart. The Nenana is a conglomeration of gravels derived from the Alaska Range, shed as the mountains were progressively uplifted over the past five or six million years. The formation is as much as 4000 feet thick in the vicinity of Healy. It is chiefly found north of the Alaska Range, tucked under the chin of the mountains like a bib catching the crumbs of their erosion.

The Park's next oldest group of sedimentary rocks is called the Usibelli Group. This group is comprised of five separate formations of sandstone, shale, conglomerate, and coal, the tops of which have been lightly peppered with a bed of hot ash. Fossils found within these rocks include the relatives and forebears of today's sequoia, pine, oak, and elm. These fossils, along with potassium-argon radiometric dating, constrain the group's age between the Eocene (about 50 million years ago) to Miocene (8 million years ago). Streamflow patterns preserved in the rock's fabric show that sediments were carried in from the north (*toward* today's Alaska Range), suggesting that a basin had formed where the Alaska Range foothills now stand. Since deposition, the rocks have been tipped (but not badly damaged) by the uprising of the Alaska Range.

The coal formation has been mined since its discovery in 1898, and is now used, among other things, to generate electricity in Fairbanks. At four most every morning a coal train pulls through Denali Park Depot and alongside Morino Campground, headed south on its way to Anchorage and on to the Orient. Morino was always my base camp because it was convenient, not to mention free. I could have sworn that the train regularly come not near, but through my tent.

The third (and for the time-being, final) sedimentary formation that we'll discuss is, geologically, perhaps the most interesting on the Park's north side. The Cantwell Formation is slightly older than the Usibelli Group, about 40 to 75 million years old, straddling the Mesozoic/Cenozoic border. It is found scattered along an east-west line near the Denali Park road, in thicknesses which in places total 5000 feet. The lower half of the Cantwell is a series of sedimentary rocks—a hodge-podge of limestone, chert, sandstone, quartzite, and whatnot. Sources for these sediments are not as well known as for the previously discussed Nenana and Usibelli units. The sediment was dumped into a basin that is now outlined by two faults that run east-west, the Hines Creek and the McKinley faults.

More about these faults later, but first let's look at the volcanics that make up the upper part of the Cantwell Formation; these are a very different

Coal mining near Denali National Park.

Photo courtesy of the University of Alaska airbanks, Alaska and Polar Regions Dept., the Elmer E. Rasmuson Library.

kind of rock—the second of our three basic types.

After a long day of shuttle-bus riding, after your hundredth stop to look at yet another caribou on the distant horizon, there is nothing like a brisk walk to wake you up. At Polychrome, grab your coat and stroll along the road east from the bus stop. Imagine that it is 56 million years ago; magma is welling up and splashing out upon the sedimentary layers of the lower Cantwell. That magma formed the upper half of the Cantwell Formation, which today consists of many thousands of feet of brightly colored volcanic rocks. These are the first substantial igneous rocks we've yet encountered.

The foothills south of Polychrome Pass offer an excellent example of these Cantwell volcanics—brilliant bands of yellow, orange, lavender, white, black, and buff rocks. This wide array of volcanic material in the upper Cantwell includes basalt, andesite, and rhyolite, each with its differing chemical composition, each adding to the variety of colors we now see. The layers were once roughly horizontal, but they have since been tipped this way and that by the emergence of the Alaska Range.

24

Cantwell Formation on
Cathedral Mountain.

At the same time that the Cantwell lavas were being extruded to the surface around Polychrome Pass, magma that rose but never reached the surface intruded rocks to the south. This material cooled slowly in great underground pockets which geologists call plutons, to form the large crystals of quartz, biotite, and feldspar that together make up granite and granodiorite. These pockets have since been uncovered by erosion, and are now recognized as the very core of the high Alaska Range—the Ruth, Kahiltna, Cathedral, and McKinley plutons. Collectively they have been called the McKinley sequence granites. The line of contact between the light-colored McKinley granite and the dark rock into which it originally intruded—the sedimentary 'flysch' that we will discuss shortly—is vividly exposed as a black-and-white slash across the North Peak of Mount McKinley.

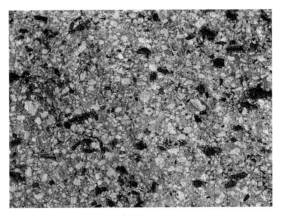

Igneous intrusive rock in Sunset Canyon, showing feldspar and biotite crystals.

The same stark relationship between the flysch and the intruding granite of the Ruth pluton enhances an already staggeringly beautiful plane ride down the length of the Ruth Glacier's Great Gorge. Looking out the window at the walls of the Gorge, one can easily imagine magma squeezing into blocks of the flysch, creating an underground chamber that slowly cooled from 1100° centigrade. And now, after a million years of uplift and erosion, the rock exists in a world of windswept granite spires and grumbling glaciers—unspeakably different than the place of birth: fire turned to ice.

Biotite flakes from these McKinley sequence granites have yielded radiometric dates in a very tight cluster just under 60 million years, about the same age as the Cantwell volcanics. Another intrusive igneous rock is the Foraker pluton, but it is significantly younger—38 million years. The neighboring McGonagall pluton lies diagonally across a valley formed by the McKinley Fault. The McGonagall is also dated at 38 million years, and precisely duplicates the Foraker's chemical signature of a healthy granodiorite, indicating that the two plutons were originally emplaced as a single body of igneous rock.

The flysch mentioned earlier bears closer inspection, as it plays a pivotal role in our evolving story of Alaskan geology—and it will serve to introduce our third and final rock type, the metamorphics. With some regret I have to report that the flysch is really a rather ugly rock. Brown, brown, with a bit more brown thrown in for good measure. The flysch is sedimentary, composed of endless sheets of mud and dirty sand, deposited during the second half of the Mesozoic in a huge underwater basin that extended southwest through what is now Denali National Park. The fabric of these sheets suggests that the mud and sand were flushed into place by furious underwater currents called turbidity flows, sweeping along the sea floor like great sandstorms.

After deposition, some of the flysch was intensely deformed. Torn, stapled by thrust faults, mutilated, compressed, and sometimes heated until it could take no more, the rock was transformed first into slate, then phyllite; some progressed to schist, and finally to gneiss—metamorphic rocks, our third basic group. From the old muds and sand, new minerals appeared: kyanite, sillimanite, staurolite. The height of this metamorphic activity seems to have occurred about 100 million years ago. The great quantities of sediment, the hectic rates of deposition, the terrible angst of the metamorphism all bespeak great goings-on in the world around Denali at that time. These pleasures of the flysch will be described in more graphic detail in the final chapter.

There remains one more group of rocks that deserves honorable mention—the exquisite schists that form the cliffs of the lower Nenana River Gorge and the walls of the Savage River as it flows past Mount Margaret. The schists, all silvery with mica, flash and twist in the sun like a single-minded school of fish. Eons ago, under intense heat and pressure, atoms within this rock realigned themselves into new crystals of amphibole, quartz, and muscovite. The plane of alignment of the individual crystals is called foliation, and is visible to the eye as fine striations along the edges of a hand-held sample.

OPPOSITE:
Dark sedimentary flysch capping peaks above the lighter granite of the Ruth Pluton, in the Great Gorge of the Ruth Glacier.

Schists of the Yukon-Tanana Crystalline Terrane. The original parallel lines of the foliation have been folded, faulted, and interlayered with quartz.

These rocks were formerly known as the Birch Creek Schist. But early attempts to correlate the schists at Denali with those found at Birch Creek northeast of Fairbanks have not proven reliable; consequently these metamorphic rocks are now lumped under an accurate (though clumsy) moniker: the Yukon-Tanana Crystalline Terrane. In general, they are found north of the Hines Creek Fault. The parent rocks from which the schists were formed appear to have been a wide variety of volcanic and sedimentary formations transformed to schist during mid-Paleozoic time. Their history is one of intense and multiple deformation. Original planes of foliation have since been twisted into increasingly complicated and eye-dazzling patterns.

STRUCTURE

On June 27, 1912, Professor Herschel Parker, Belmore Browne, and Merl LaVoy came agonizingly close to being the first men to reach the true summit of Mount McKinley. With the South Peak no more than hailing distance away, the men were beaten back by a sudden storm. Browne later wrote,

> Professor Parker's barometer at last registered 20,000 feet. . . . The last period of our climb is like the memory of an evil dream. LaVoy was completely lost in the ice mist, and Professor Parker's frosted form was an indistinct blur above me. As the blood congealed in my fingers I went back to LaVoy. He was getting the end of the gale's whiplash, and when I yelled that we couldn't stand the wind he agreed that it was suicide to try. I turned to Professor Parker and yelled, "The game's up; we've got to get down!"

Mount McKinley's summit might as well have been the far side of the moon. The climbing world had experienced other earlier disappointments. First there was Dr. Frederick C. Cook's celebrated (but untrue) claim of having reached the summit in eight days during August 1906. Then, four years later, the Sourdough expedition from Fairbanks did successfully climb the lower North Peak, but the achievement was obscured when their leader Tom Lloyd inaccurately boasted that they had also made it to the higher South Peak.

And now the Parker-Browne expedition was in retreat. Recuperating at Cache Creek two days after stepping off the Muldrow Glacier, the men were stunned by a rumbling that shook the entire Alaska Range. The ground around them pitched like a ship at sea. As they watched, the western flank of Mount Brooks was swept clean by a miles-long avalanche. A cloud of snow four thousand feet high swept over the climbers in an icy sixty-mile-an-hour blast.

Karstens Ridge.

Summit or no summit, the men, still alive, counted themselves lucky to be off the mountain.

A year later, in 1913, another group of Fairbanks climbers led by Harry Karstens did reach Mount McKinley's summit. Karstens not only reached the summit, but also became Denali National Park's first superintendent. Karstens' group followed the route recommended by Professor Parker, but they were baffled by the massive jumble of broken ice occupying a ridge that had been smooth and easily traversed the year before. Then they remembered the professor's story of the July 6 earthquake.

Alaska is hardly a stranger to earthquakes. The Good Friday quake of 1964, centered just east of Anchorage and north of Prince William Sound, registered 8.6 on the Richter scale and was felt over half a million square miles. A 1958 earthquake at Glacier Bay National Park dropped 40 million cubic yards of rock from a 3000-foot perch into Lituya Bay; the resulting wave rushed across the bay at 130 miles an hour and swashed 1720 feet up a wall opposite the landslide.

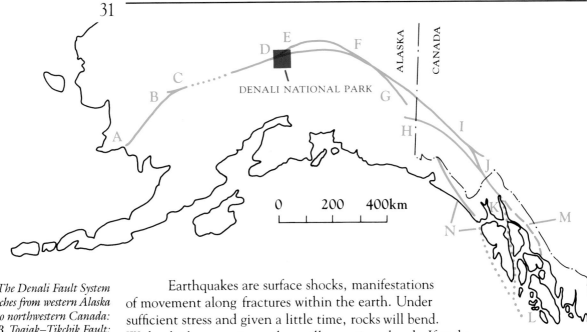

The Denali Fault System stretches from western Alaska into northwestern Canada: A–B, Togiak–Tikchik Fault; B–C, Holitna Fault; C–D, Farewell segment; D–F, McKinley segment; E–F, Hines Creek segment; F–I, Shakwak segment; G, Totschunda Fault; H–J, Duke River Fault; I–J, Dalton Fault; J–K, Chilkat River Fault; K–L, Chatham Strait Fault; M, Coast Range megalineament; N, Fairweather–Queen Charlotte Fault zone.
(After M. A. Lanphere, *Can J Earth Sci*, v. 15, 1978.)

Earthquakes are surface shocks, manifestations of movement along fractures within the earth. Under sufficient stress and given a little time, rocks will bend. With a little more stress, they will sometimes break. If rocks along such a fracture were subsequently to move relative to one another, then the fracture would be called a fault. And, if the movement along the fault is strong enough, we on the surface experience it as an earthquake.

Structural geology is the study of rock behavior: given a particular stress, why does this rock bend and that rock break? The structural geology of Denali most basically concerns itself with three fundamental features: the Denali Fault system, the great thrust faults south of the Park, and the uplift of the Alaska range. We will consider each of these in turn.

Faults are found throughout Alaska. In 1957, Pierre St. Amand pored over the maps of his day and concluded that a gigantic single fault stretched along a great curve from southeast Alaska all the way to the Bering Sea—this he called the Denali Fault system. Individual fault segments had been recognized since the turn of the century, but no one before had connected the dots to form such a sweeping single system. For years after that, geologists postulated that southern Alaska had moved huge distances as a single block along this fault system, sliding north and west relative to the rest of North America.

The McKinley Fault—a segment of the Denali Fault system—runs right through the Park's back yard. The fault, by breaking up the rocks through which it cuts, has focused the forces of erosion to carve a discontinuous east-west valley along the south side of the Alaska Range, from the Parks Highway near Cantwell through Anderson Pass. From this pass westward, the fault cuts along the northern Alaska Range; indeed, the fault lies exactly at the base of the clean-shaven face of the Wickersham Wall.

The McKinley Fault dissected and displaced the Foraker and McGonagall plutons, which were originally intruded as a single mass of granite straddling the fault. Reconstruction of the movement of these plutons suggests about twenty-five miles of horizontal motion along the McKinley Fault since the granite was formed 38 million years ago.

A strike-slip fault cuts two blocks of land, sliding one block past the other. Surface features like streams or glaciers are offset by the fault.

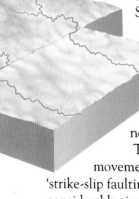

Geologists have also looked at the McKinley Fault's influence on the path and shapes of glaciers. A few—the Muldrow, Peters, Straightaway, Foraker, and Chedotlothna—flow from the Alaska Range north across the McKinley Fault. Each is deflected eastward by the fault for at least a few miles before escaping and again turning north. This zig-zag arrangement reflects the fact that the glaciers' source areas high in the Alaska Range are being dragged westward, while the lower segments of the glaciers lying north of the fault are being carried to the east.

The McKinley Fault, then, demonstrates a degree of horizontal movement. Geologists call this sort of horizontal or side-by-side movement 'strike-slip faulting.' A person standing on either side of the fault would (over considerable time) watch rocks on the other side move to the right. Thus the McKinley Fault is properly described as a right-lateral strike-slip fault.

Some sections of the Denali Fault system have been better studied than

Cantwell Formation above the East Fork of the Toklat River. A dike here intruded the Cantwell, and was subsequently broken when the Cantwell was folded. Each block of the dike rotated as layers of the sedimentary rock slid over one another during folding.

others. Both the direction and rate of movement have been well documented along segments of the system in southeast Alaska. The Fairweather Fault at Lituya Bay, for example, has been galloping along at a little more than two inches a year for the past 100,000 years. If the McKinley Fault were moving this fast, Los Angeles would be within the Park boundaries in another 50 million years. Heaven forbid.

This, however, is considerably faster than rates determined for the McKinley Fault as it has sheared past the Foraker pluton over the last 38 million years. Surveyors' triangulations in the area of the Nenana River show no strike-slip movement along the fault—not even a little bit—since first being measured in 1942.

Scarp of the McKinley Strand of the Denali Fault where it crosses Bull Creek.

The theory of the entire Denali Fault system moving as a single block has begun to erode over the past few years. The 'fault system' is still a useful concept, relating its component fault segments to each other in a general sense. But as all of the segments are studied more closely, we begin to realize that each fault within the system has its own character and peculiar history.

The McKinley Fault gives little evidence of horizontal movement in the last few thousand years. For instance, from Cantwell to Anderson Pass, most streambeds run straight across the fault without the telltale lateral deflections of their channels that would suggest recent strike-slip motion. Some geologists have even revised estimates of lateral movement along the McKinley Fault to as little as tens of miles.

The McKinley Fault has been moving, but its motion appears to be slower and more complex than the purely horizontal movement that geologists initially proposed. On a hike from Cantwell to Eielson, I scrambled over scarps formed by the McKinley Fault in the Bull Creek Basin. The scarps (which are breaks in the surface along which the fault has moved) are reasonably fresh, but most seemed to demonstrate vertical—not horizontal—movement, sometimes south side down, sometimes north side down.

The Hines Creek Fault is another of the Park's major structural features, considered an older part of the Denali Fault system. It runs roughly east-west, in a line that passes near the Denali Park Depot area, westward beyond the Teklanika Campground. To the north of this fault, one finds schists of the Yukon-Tanana Crystalline Terrane; to the south lies everything else—the flysch, the Cantwell Formation, and the McKinley granites.

The upper block of land is sliding up over the lower block along a thrust fault. These faults suggest an environment dominated by lateral compression.

Because the rock formations on either side of the fault are so radically different, some geologists have considered the Hines Creek Fault to be a major boundary along which a great deal of movement has taken place over the years. To the east of the Park, a 95-million-year-old granite intrudes across the fault without subsequently being cut by it; thus the fault in that location hasn't been active at least since late Mesozoic time. If the Hines Creek Fault is a major boundary, its heyday of activity must have been many years ago.

Nonetheless, along Hines Creek near the Park Headquarters, the fault does separate schist from the Cantwell Formation, suggesting movement more recent than late Mesozoic. Fine striations in the sheared faces of the rocks, called slickensides, argue for at least some recent movement along the Hines Creek Fault, oriented vertically, not horizontally.

The McKinley and Hines Creek faults give examples of side-to-side and up-and-down motion along fault planes. Another mode of faulting is also found within and around the Park, and has played a major role in shaping the landscape of Denali. 'Thrust' faults are formed when rocks on one side of a fault are compressed so forcefully that one block rides up over another. The Talkeetna Thrust Fault is found south of the Alaska Range, where the leading edge of the Talkeetna Mountains rode up onto rocks to the northwest. A similar fault, called the Honolulu Thrust, is found a bit farther northwest, along the route of the highway from Honolulu (AK) to Cantwell.

These thrusts occurred in the middle of the Cretaceous period, about 100 million years ago. They are characterized by a zone of finely ground-up rock, and are bordered by formations which at a geologist's first glance seem totally out of place. The Cretaceous forces that created the Talkeetna and Honolulu thrust faults were associated with a great deal of deformation well beyond the faults themselves. Metamorphic changes occurred in a wide belt of rocks throughout south-central Alaska during the middle Cretaceous.

The forces within the earth responsible for faults can also build mountains. Uplift of the Alaska Range seems to have begun in earnest within the last sixty million years, most of it being accomplished even more recently. This uplift has not been nearly so devastating as the previous Cretaceous episode of compression, thrust faulting, and metamorphism. The Nenana Gravels were tilted a bit, the Cantwell Formation was even folded, but no metamorphism occurred.

OPPOSITE:
*East face of Mt. McKinley.
The Wickersham Wall, with
its trace of the Denali Fault,
is in shadow on the right.*

The Alaska Range is young, still rising as far as we know. But even as the mountains grow taller, erosion whittles away at their flanks—glaciers, rock falls, streams all busy taking the range apart, grain by grain, boulder by boulder. So far, the mountains are winning. Mount McKinley stands higher above its surrounding plain than most other mountains on earth. Geologists like to explain that the granites of Mount McKinley are less dense than some of the neighboring formations, allowing the mountain to float a bit higher on the earth's surface. Perhaps. But there are a lot of similar granites in the world that haven't been so blessed with buoyancy. As we will see in the next chapter, Denali is at the very apex of an earth-moving and mountain-building episode that is giving a facelift to all of western North America. So why is the mountain so high? I honestly don't know.

TECTONICS

He conjured in his dreams a world where the rocks were hot and moving, where quakes and volcanoes turned shales to schist, granites to gneiss, limestone to marble, sandstone to quartz, where continents sank and rose like kelp on the tide.

Jim Crace, *Continent*

Continents flowing like kelp. Before the mid-1960s, most folks would have scoffed at the idea. But with the introduction and general acceptance of the theory of plate tectonics, geologists have been forced to rethink their entire understanding of the earth.

Some of the earliest evidence for the theory of plate tectonics was found on the bottom of the ocean. For years, oceanographers had noted but could not explain a system of ridges that runs like a great mountain chain along most of the world's seafloors, in a pattern that encircles the earth like stitches on a baseball cover. In the 1950s geologists began to look more closely at these ridges and realized that magma is welling up out of them.

Between the earth's surface and its inner core is a hot liquid zone called the mantle, made up of molten magma. When this magma is extruded at sea-floor ridges, it freezes into rock and is pushed laterally in both directions away from the ridge. This layer of rock according to plate tectonics theory is an ocean-floor plate, and is floating on the mantle.

OPPOSITE:
Alaska Range Foothills.

Rocks of the oceanic plates, usually basalt or one of its cousins, tend to be quite heavy, with densities a little more than three times that of water. This is in contrast to rocks typically found within continental plates, which have an average density only about two-and-a-half times that of water. These density

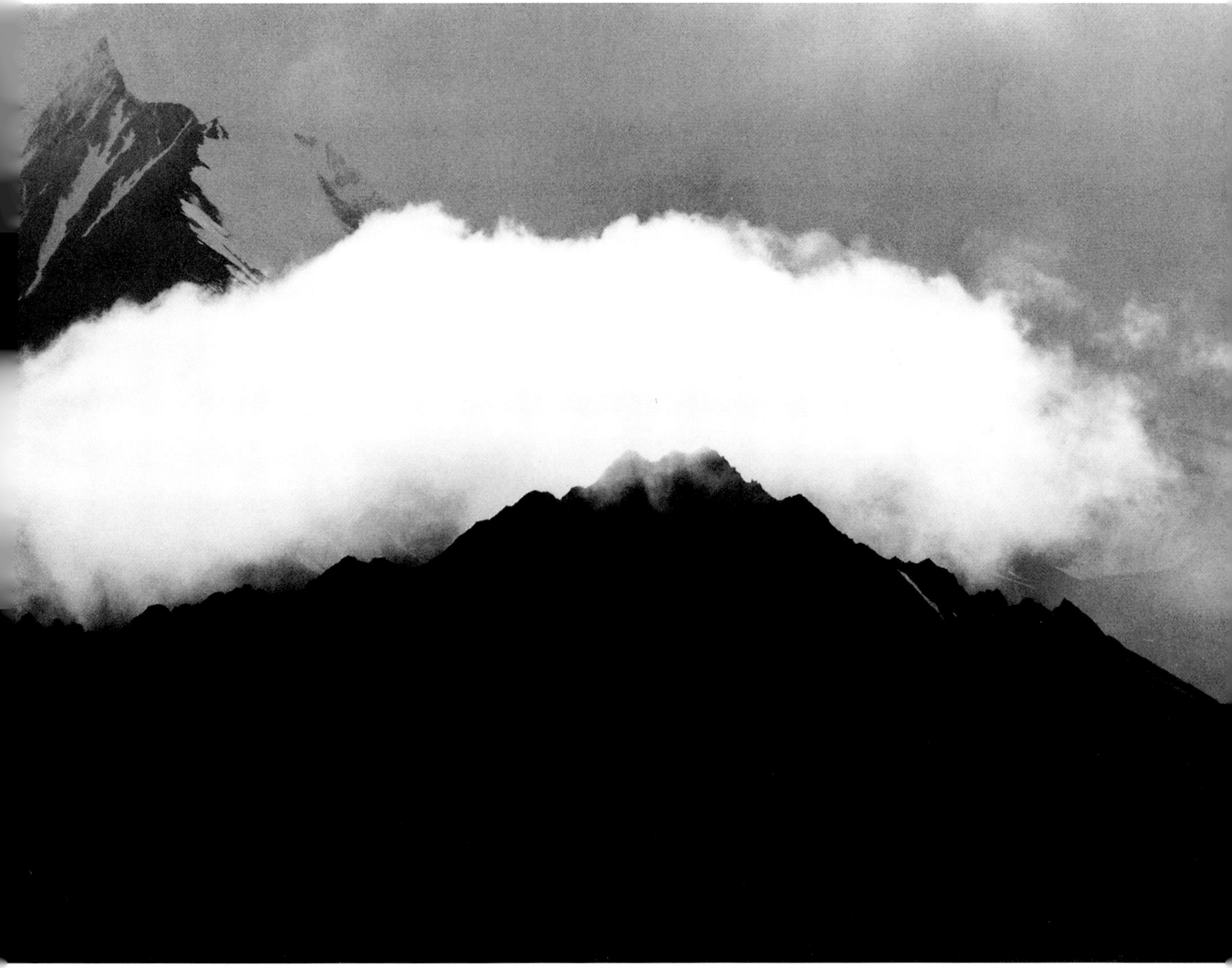

differences may seem small, even inconsequential, but when applied to a few million cubic miles of rock, they become staggeringly important.

As the heavier oceanic plates spread away from the ridges, they eventually collide with, and usually dive beneath lighter continental rocks. On the other hand, when two continental plates collide, neither is likely to sink beneath the other. Instead they rear up one against the other, forming mountains like the Appalachians and the Himalayas.

Plate tectonics is an idea that has revolutionized the science of geology at least as much as the discovery of DNA advanced the study of lions and tigers. Suddenly geologists had a theory that could tie up many loose ends: applicable to problems that concern the greatest mountain ranges to tiniest crystallization patterns.

Geologists quickly divvied up the modern world into fifteen or twenty major plates and quite a few smaller ones. North America is a single large plate; nowadays, so is most of the Pacific Ocean. These two plates are moving relative to one another—sliding side-by-side along California's San Andreas Fault and Southeast Alaska's Fairweather Fault. Indeed, large faults are often used to define plate boundaries.

Farther north, the Pacific Plate is diving beneath North America along the Aleutian Trench, just south and seaward of the Aleutian Islands. The plane along which an oceanic plate bends beneath a continental plate is called a *subduction zone*. The ocean floor acts, then, as a gigantic conveyor belt—forming at a mid-oceanic ridge, moving laterally until it is forced to dive back into the earth's mantle.

As the Pacific Plate slides back into the earth, it drags along the underside of Alaska, setting off earthquakes like an on-going shower of sparks. For years, geophysicists have been plotting the exact location and depth of these earthquakes. Their maps show that earthquake foci (called hypocenters) are spread out along a plane that slants back down into the earth—exactly marking the location and angle of an oceanic plate as it subducts beneath the more buoyant continental plate.

Once the oceanic plate descends to a depth where the earth's interior is sufficiently hot—perhaps three or four hundred miles down—it is remelted into the mantle. Lighter continental material that has been dragged down with the oceanic plate also melts, becoming buoyant enough to then rise back to the surface, to form volcanic chains like the Aleutian Islands.

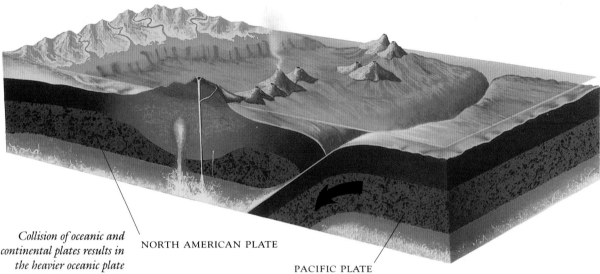

NORTH AMERICAN PLATE

PACIFIC PLATE

Collision of oceanic and continental plates results in the heavier oceanic plate diving ('subducting') beneath the continental plate. Sediments are dragged down with the oceanic plate and eventually reach depths with sufficient heat to cause melting; the molten material rises back to the surface, forming volcanoes.

Earthquakes, faults, volcanoes—these are aspects of geology that have been studied for years and are only now better understood in light of the theory of plate tectonics. Plate tectonics in a nutshell: oceanic and continental plates playing leap-frog and bumper-cars as they slip and slide across the top of the earth's mantle.

In 1980, Peter Coney published a landmark paper suggesting that a great deal of western North America had not always been where it is now. Instead, he suggested that great landmasses had been rafted in and stuck along the continent's western margin, like mud thrown against and smeared along a wall. These landmasses he identified as 'suspect terranes': geologic provinces whose stratigraphy and structure reflected a distinctive geologic history, with abrupt faulted boundaries separating them from neighboring provinces.

Unlike a proper oceanic or continental plate, a suspect terrane does not usually float directly on the earth's mantle; instead it hitches a ride on top of, or at the edge of a plate. The Pacific Plate could carry a number of suspect terranes on its back. A continental plate like North America could (and apparently does) contain many smaller suspect terranes.

Geologic theoreticians had a field day. Alaska and the nearby Yukon were quickly diced into fifty separate terranes. The idea was that each terrane had been formed somewhere else and was carried northward on the back of the Pacific Plate (or on its once-upon-a-time subdivisions, called the Kula and Farallon plates). As the great conveyor belt rolled north, these lighter terranes were scraped off the subducting oceanic plate, and were docked against the southern edge of Alaska.

Where did these suspect terranes come from? What continent spawned these orphan terranes? How were the terranes loaded onto the back of the Pacific Plate in the first place? Geologists haven't gotten that far yet, but the subscience of paleomagnetics offers some insight. We've known for a while that, as rocks are formed, they inherit a magnetic orientation parallel to the earth's poles. The magnetic field is oriented not only north-south, but also inclines into the earth's surface at a particular angle for any given latitude. By examining a rock's magnetic signature, geologists have learned to estimate how far from the North or South pole a given rock was at the time of its magnetization. Pretty crafty. The paleomagnetic fingerprints of the terranes in the Denali area suggest separate origins of each of its component terranes, just south of the equator.

In simplest terms, Denali National Park can be thought of as three regions, each made up of a number of suspect terranes: land north of the Hines Creek Fault, land south of the McKinley Fault, and the land between these two faults. The northern third of the Park, lying north of the Hines Creek Fault, is made up of the Yukon-Tenana terrane. This terrane, composed largely of Paleozoic metamorphic rocks like schist and phyllite, was probably a well-established part of Alaska by mid-Mesozoic time.

OPPOSITE:
Alaska and Northwest Canada have been subdivided into many 'terranes', each accreted to the North American continent as they were carried up from the south on the back of the Pacific Plate. AAC, Arctic Alaska; AAD, Delong Mountains subterrane; AAE, Endicott Mountains subterrane; AAH, Hammond subterrane; AAN, North Slope subterrane; AGM, Angayucham; ALX, Alexander; CCK, Cache Creek; CGH, Chugach; DIL, Dillinger; EAS, Eastern composite (Kootenay, Slide Mtn, McLeod, Cassiar, Monashee); GNW, Goodnews; INN, Innoko; KYK, Koyukuk; LVG, Livengood; MNA, Minchumina; NXF, Nixon Fork; NYK, Nyack; PCP, Porcupine; PEN, Peninsular; PMW, Pingston, McKinley and Windy combined; PRW, Prince William; QNL, Quesnellia; RUB, Ruby; SEW, Seward Peninsula; STK, Stikinia; TKU, Taku; TOG, Togiak; TOZ, Tozitna; TRA, Tracy Arm; WRN, Wrangellia; YAK, Yakutat; YKT, Yukon–Tanana; YOK, York. (After Stone and Wallace, *Episodes*, v. 10, 1987.)

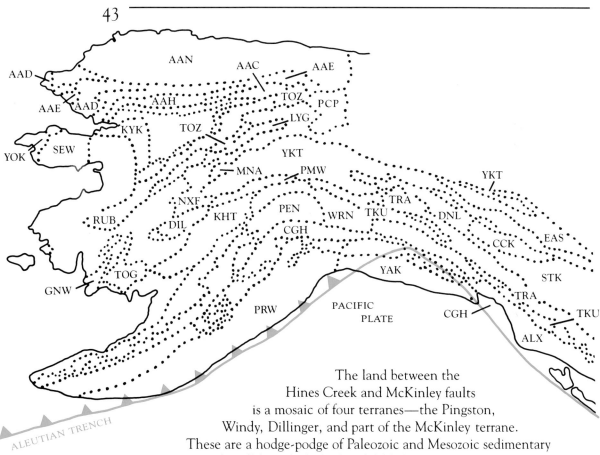

The land between the
Hines Creek and McKinley faults
is a mosaic of four terranes—the Pingston,
Windy, Dillinger, and part of the McKinley terrane.
These are a hodge-podge of Paleozoic and Mesozoic sedimentary
and igneous rocks, all heavily faulted and folded.

The third region, south of the McKinley Fault, requires a little more
explanation. At the end of the Mesozoic, say 70 or 80 million years ago, the
Pacific Ocean lapped at what is now the southern boundary of Denali Park,
somewhere near the McKinley Fault. Sailing up from the south, carried by the
north-moving Pacific Plate, was a huge landmass that geologists have dubbed the
Talkeetna Superterrane. Apparently, the Talkeetna was a prefab composite of a

number of smaller terranes—Wrangellia, Peninsular, Maclaren, and Alexander to name a few.

As the Superterrane approached Alaska, tremendous quantities of sediment washed down from the two landmasses and filled the basin that remained between them. These sediments were to become the Jurassic/Cretaceous flysch, which was subsequently crumpled into tortuous folds by the Superterrane as it finally collided with Alaska. Before grinding to a stop between 65 and 55 million years ago, the Talkeetna Superterrane was thrust up over parts of continental Alaska. That event is now recorded by the Talkeetna and Honolulu thrust faults.

The Talkeetna Superterrane acted as a bulldozer, pushing other blocks of land ahead of it. These were smaller suspect terranes—the Chulitna, Susitna, and others—and are found as slivers sandwiched between the Talkeetna Superterrane and older Alaska, near the south end of Denali Park. The Chulitna is a relatively small terrane, only fifty miles in length, that includes a distinctive Paleozoic-age ocean-bottom sequence of rocks called an ophiolite complex, unlike any of its neighbors. The Chulitna is among the better studied suspect terranes; indeed it helped Peter Coney initially formulate his ideas on suspect terranes.

Following the arrival of the Talkeetna Superterrane, the Chugach and Prince William terranes were in turn accreted to southern Alaska. All of these accretions have led to emplacement of land—including Denali National Park—where once there was only ocean. With each accretion, the North American continent has grown a little bit larger.

As the terranes piled up, the Pacific-North American subduction zone at some point had to jump south to its current location which begins just beyond the Aleutian Islands. This jump obviously involved tremendous geologic forces, but the mechanisms by which it occurred remain very much a mystery. An area called the Yakutat Block is currently sliding along the Fairweather Fault, docking to the south of the Wrangell Mountains. Geologists speculate that this collision is causing the eastern end of the Pacific-North American subduction zone to reorganize, possibly to skip farther south once again.

The last few paragraphs have been peppered with a suspicious number of apparently's, allegedly's, and possibly's. And for good reason. I'd sooner take my chances in a Fourth Street Saturday-night barroom brawl, than get caught between any two geologists trying to rationally discuss the ideas that have just been presented. There is precious little agreement about the details of timing, sequence, or significance of all these events. The Hines Creek and McKinley faults may or may not have been major terrane boundaries, and may or may not have experienced many hundreds of miles of movement. There may be fifty terranes or there may be just three of four. The earth beneath Denali Park may be stable old continental crust, or it may be a composite of many suspect terranes.

Everybody has an opinion and nobody is budging—not yet anyway. Alaskan geology is still a wide-open game. Only a fraction of the land has been studied in serious detail, and basic geologic mapping remains to be done throughout the state. Major papers are published based on two days in the field, one of which is restricted by bad weather. Alaskan geology is in that tipsy, exciting phase of youthful discoveries and shiny new theories. Little wonder that not everyone agrees.

DENALI. THE HIGH ONE. The mountain will always seduce my curiosity, will always be greater than the sum of my knowledge of its geology. From my tent door at Crystal Creek I watch dawn arrive, swirling like vapor along the northeast flank of the mountain, all pink and promising. The Wickersham Wall looms above like a fifteen-thousand-foot wave that could break at any second; but it has been hanging there since Distant Time and probably won't come down today. Clouds are forming above Kahiltna Pass, ten or twelve layers exactly parallel to one another, spaced perhaps five hundred feet apart, lapping onto Denali. A raven flashes over my tent, headed out over the blackened ice of the Muldrow Glacier, chased by two indignant smaller birds.
Nothing has changed; he'll get away once again.

ACKNOWLEDGEMENTS

After two months in the field at Denali, I developed a tremendous respect for the geologists who have done the real work that is presented in this book. Bela Csejtey, Biff Reed, David Stone, Wyatt Gilbert, and Art Grantz generously contributed time, pointed out important publications, and helped steer me through the current thinking on Alaska geology. George Wagner, Chief Naturalist with the National Park Service in Denali, was consistently ethusiastic and actively supportive of this project. The folks at the Alaska Natural History Association (now known as Alaska Geographic) paved the ways that otherwise could have been rocky. Ruth Reitmeier was everything that a writer could wish of an editor: clear-thinking, incisive and unabashed. Russ Johnson was the perfect co-pilot, never letting me pass up an opportunity for just one more aerial photograph. And Phil Brease, Denali Park's resident geologist, was good enough to haul me from Cantwell to Eielson, through nine days of wet feet, great scenery, and unflagging good spirits. My thanks to you all.

OPPOSITE:
Cantwell Formation with dikes, above the East Fork of the Toklat River.

FURTHER READING

Bundtzen, Thomas K. A History of Mining in the Kantishna Hills. *Alaska Journal*, pp. 151-161. Spring 1978.

Collier, Michael, *Sculpted by Ice: Glaciers and the Alaska Landscape*. Alaska Geographic, Anchorage. 2004

Coney, P., D. L. Jones, and J. W. H. Monger. Cordilleran Suspect Terranes. *Nature* 288: 329-333. November 1980.

Csejtey, B., D. P. Cox, R. C. Evarts, G. D. Stricker, and H. L. Foster. The Cenozoic Denali Fault System and the Cretaceous Accretionary Development of Southern Alaska. *Journal of Geophysical Research*, 87:B5, 3741-3754. 1982.

Hillhouse, John W. Accretion of Southern Alaska. *Tectonophysics* 139: 107-122. 1987.

Jones, D. L., A. Cox, P. Coney, and M. Beck. The Growth of Western North America. *Scientific American*, pp. 70-84. November 1982.

48

Jones, D. L., N. J. Silberling, W. Gilbert, and P. Coney. Character, Distribution, and the Tectonic Significance of Accretionary Terranes in the Central Alaska Range. *Journal of Geophysical Research*, 87:B5, 3709–3717. 1982.

Jones, D. L., N. J. Silberling, P. J. Coney, and G. Plafker. Lithotectonic Terrane Map of Alaska (West of the 141st Meridian). U.S. Geological Survey Map MF-1874-A. 1987.

Lanphere, M. A., and B. L. Reed. The McKinley Sequence of Granitic Rocks: A Key Element in the Accretionary History of Southern Alaska. *Journal of Geophysical Research*, 90:B13, 11, 413–11, 430. 1985.

Moore, Terris. *Mt. McKinley: The Pioneer Climbs*. The Mountaineers, Seattle, for the University of Alaska. 1981.

Nelson, Richard K. *Make Prayers to the Raven: A Koyukon View of the Northern Forest*. University of Chicago Press, Chicago. 1983.

Reed, John C. The Mount Eielson District, Alaska. *U.S. Geological Survey Bulletin* 849-D. 1933.

St. Amand, Pierre. Geological and Geophysical Synthesis of the Tectonics of Portions of British Columbia, The Yukon Territory, and Alaska. *Bulletin of the Geological Society of America*, 68: 1343–1370. 1957.

Stone, D. B., and W. K. Wallace. A Geological Framework of Alaska. *Episodes* 10:4, 283–289. 1987

Wahrhaftig, Clyde. Schists of the Central Alaska Range. *U.S. Geological Survey Bulletin 1254-E*. 1968.

Wahrhaftig, C., J. A. Wolfe, and E. B. Leopold. The Coal-Bearing Group in the Nenana Coal Field, Alaska. *U.S. Geological Survey Bulletin 1274-D*. 1969.

Wahrhaftig, C., D. L. Turner, F. R. Weber, and T. E. Smith. Nature and Timing or Movement of Hines Creek Strand of Denali Fault System, Alaska. *Geology*, pp. 463–466. August 1975.